Thank you so much for reading my book!

My name is Debra Shawn Daubenspeck. I was born and raised in Orlando, Florida, but now reside in the Sandhills of North Carolina with my husband Alan. I am a professional singer, recording artist, real estate photographer, cancer survivor, homemaker, mother of two, and now, author.

Music, photography, and attention to small details have always been important to me. I've been a professional singer for over thirty years and a real estate photographer for the last ten. After being diagnosed with cervical cancer in 2016 and completing my cancer treatments, I experienced a lot of anxiety and depression. I started collecting Barbie dolls and accessories to help with this, and found setting up scenes and photographing them was very therapeutic and relaxing for me. As I shared the photos with close friends and family, I got the same feedback: "I love this!" Then my husband suggested to me, "You should do a book!" What started as a hobby of mine turned into this project, called *The Life of Dolls*.

In this book, you will find scenes of everyday life staged with my personal dolls, furniture, and props. After moving all of my photography equipment and dolls into our den, I set up a folding table where I started building the scenes from scratch. Starting with poster board or framed art as a backdrop, I added flooring and then the furniture. Last (and most difficult) was posing the dolls and having to balance some of the standing dolls while trying to capture the perfect angle with my camera. The collapse of one doll would create a domino effect in the very small space.

I would like to dedicate this book to my mom and dad, for buying me so many great dolls as a child. Also, to my sisters, LaJuana, Teresa, and Fonda, whom I played dolls with as a little girl, and my brother, Bobby, who first introduced me to G.I. Joe. An extra big THANK YOU to my sister, Fonda, for her gift of over thirty unopened collectible dolls, and to Teresa for her gift of over forty dolls, furniture, and accessories.

I hope you enjoy looking through the pages as much as I enjoyed creating them!

—Debra Shawn Daubenspeck

www.mascotbooks.com

The Life of Dolls

For more information, please contact:
Mascot Books
620 Herndon Parkway, Suite 320
Herndon, VA 20170
info@mascotbooks.com

Library of Congress Control Number: 2020905441

CPSIA Code: PRT0520A
ISBN-13: 978-1-64543-594-5

Printed in the United States

THE LIFE OF
DOLLS

Debra Shawn Daubenspeck

Breakfast

Movie Night

The Artist

Bath Time

Western Girl

Pop
Band

Wedding Day

Day at the Park

Sports Car

Tea Party

Jazz Singer

Beauty Salon

Laundry Day

Game Night

Slumber Party

Helicopter Ride

Tropical Island Vacation

Yoga Class

New Bike

Busking in the City

Office Work

Valentine's Day

Saint Patrick's Day

Easter Sunday

4th of July

Halloween Party

Thanksgiving Day

Christmas

The CAST

Hollywood Gals

Awards Night

Grand Entrance   Ballerina